# SCIENTOLOGY
*Improving Life in a Troubled World*

Founded and developed by L. Ron Hubbard, Scientology is an applied religious philosophy which offers an exact route through which anyone can regain the truth and simplicity of his spiritual self.

Scientology consists of specific axioms that define the underlying causes and principles of existence and a vast area of observations in the humanities, a philosophic body that literally applies to the entirety of life.

This broad body of knowledge resulted in two applications of the subject: first, a technology for man to increase his spiritual awareness and attain the freedom sought by many great philosophic teachings; and, second, a great number of fundamental principles men can use to improve their lives. In fact, in this second application, Scientology offers nothing less than practical methods to better *every* aspect of our existence—means to create new ways of life. And from this comes the subject matter you are about to read.

Compiled from the writings of L. Ron Hubbard, the data presented here is but one of the tools which can be found in *The Scientology Handbook*. A comprehensive guide, the handbook contains numerous applications of Scientology which can be used to improve many other areas of life.

In this booklet, the editors have augmented the data with a short introduction, practical exercises and examples of successful application.

Courses to increase your understanding and further materials to broaden your knowledge are available at your nearest Scientology church or mission, listed at the back of this booklet.

Many new phenomena about man and life are described in Scientology, and so you may encounter terms in these pages you are not familiar with. These are described the first time they appear and in the glossary at the back of the booklet.

Scientology is for use. It is a practical philosophy, something one *does*. Using this data, you *can* change conditions.

Millions of people who want to do something about the conditions they see around them have applied this knowledge. They know that life can be improved. And they know that Scientology works.

Use what you read in these pages to help yourself and others and you will too.

CHURCH OF SCIENTOLOGY INTERNATIONAL

*Why are some people ill more often than others? Why are some accident-prone? And is there a reason others live their lives on an emotional seesaw, doing well one day and badly the next?*

*There is an explanation, and it has nothing to do with the gods, fate or the position of the stars. In fact, the actual reason behind these phenomena—and their resolution—has been explained in Scientology.*

*L. Ron Hubbard was able to see through the complexities of human behavior and discover the underlying factors which explain the phenomenon of* **suppression** *in people—for it is suppression by others that causes these seemingly haphazard events. In the excerpts from his writings in this booklet, you will find out how to recognize people who wish you ill and those who should be your friends. You'll discover why some people do poorly in life and how you can help them regain their well-being. You'll learn about the mechanics behind this destructive yet commonplace situation and ways to counteract it. It is data that could actually change your life tangibly and instantly, just as it has changed the lives of others.*

# THE ANTISOCIAL PERSONALITY

There are certain characteristics and mental attitudes which cause about 20 percent of a race to oppose violently any betterment activity or group.

Such people are known to have antisocial tendencies.

When the legal or political structure of a country becomes such as to favor such personalities in positions of trust, then all the civilizing organizations of the country become suppressed and a barbarism of criminality and economic duress ensues.

Crime and criminal acts are perpetrated by antisocial personalities. Inmates of institutions commonly trace their state back to contact with such personalities.

Thus, in the fields of government, police activities and mental health, to name a few, we see that it is important to be able to detect and isolate this personality type so as to protect society and individuals from the destructive consequences attendant upon letting such have free rein to injure others.

As they only comprise 20 percent of the population and as only 2½ percent are truly dangerous, we see that with a very small amount of effort we could considerably better the state of society.

Well-known, even stellar, examples of such a personality are, of course, Napoleon and Hitler. Dillinger, Pretty Boy Floyd, Christie and other famous criminals were well-known examples of the antisocial personality. But with such a cast of characters in history we neglect the less stellar examples and do not perceive that such personalities exist in current life, very common, often undetected.

When we trace the cause of a failing business, we will inevitably discover somewhere in its ranks the antisocial personality hard at work.

*A relatively small proportion of a race, about 20 percent, possess antisocial characteristics. They cause trouble for the remaining 80 percent out of proportion to their number.*

In families which are breaking up, we commonly find one or the other of the persons involved to have such a personality.

Where life has become rough and is failing, a careful review of the area by a trained observer will detect one or more such personalities at work.

As there are 80 percent of us trying to get along and only 20 percent trying to prevent us, our lives would be much easier to live were we well informed as to the exact manifestations of such a personality. Thus, we could detect it and save ourselves much failure and heartbreak.

It is important then to examine and list the attributes of the antisocial personality. Influencing as it does the daily lives of so many, it well behooves decent people to become better informed on this subject.

# Attributes

The antisocial personality has the following attributes:

**1. He or she speaks only in very broad generalities.** "They say . . ." "Everybody thinks . . ." "Everyone knows . . ." and such expressions are in continual use, particularly when imparting rumor. When asked, "*Who* is everybody . . ." it normally turns out to be one source and from this source the antisocial person has manufactured what he or she pretends is the whole opinion of the whole society.

This is natural to them since to them all society is a large hostile generality, against the antisocial in particular.

**2. Such a person deals mainly in bad news, critical or hostile remarks, invalidation and general suppression.**

"Gossip" or "bearer of evil tidings" or "rumormonger" once described such persons.

It is notable that there is no good news or complimentary remark passed on by such a person.

**3. The antisocial personality alters, to worsen, communication when he or she relays a message or news.** Good news is stopped and only bad news, often embellished, is passed along.

Such a person also pretends to pass on "bad news" which is in actual fact invented.

**4. A characteristic, and one of the sad things about an antisocial personality, is that it does not respond to treatment or reform.**

**5. Surrounding such a personality we find cowed or ill associates or friends who, when not driven actually insane, are yet behaving in a crippled manner in life, failing, not succeeding.**

Such people make trouble for others.

When treated or educated, the near associate of the antisocial personality has no stability of gain but promptly relapses or loses his advantages of knowledge, being under the suppressive influence of the other.

Physically treated, such associates commonly do not recover in the expected time but worsen and have poor convalescences.

It is quite useless to treat or help or train such persons so long as they remain under the influence of the antisocial connection.

The largest number of insane are insane because of such antisocial connections and do not recover easily for the same reason.

Unjustly we seldom see the antisocial personality actually in an institution. Only his "friends" and family are there.

6. **The antisocial personality habitually selects the wrong target.**

If a tire is flat from driving over nails, he or she curses a companion or a noncausative source of the trouble. If the radio next door is too loud, he or she kicks the cat.

If A is the obvious cause, the antisocial personality inevitably blames B or C or D.

7. **The antisocial cannot finish a cycle of action.** Any action goes through a sequence wherein the action is begun, is continued for as long as is required and is completed as planned. In Scientology, this is called a *cycle of action*.

The antisocial becomes surrounded with incomplete projects.

8. **Many antisocial persons will freely confess to the most alarming crimes when forced to do so, but will have no faintest sense of responsibility for them.**

Their actions have little or nothing to do with their own volition. Things "just happened."

They have no sense of correct causation and particularly cannot feel any sense of remorse or shame therefore.

9. The antisocial personality supports only destructive groups and rages against and attacks any constructive or betterment group.

10. This type of personality approves only of destructive actions and fights against constructive or helpful actions or activities.

The artist in particular is often found as a magnet for persons with antisocial personalities who see in his art something which must be destroyed and covertly, "as a friend," proceed to try.

11. Helping others is an activity which drives the antisocial personality nearly berserk. Activities, however, which destroy in the name of help are closely supported.

12. The antisocial personality has a bad sense of property and conceives that the idea that anyone owns anything is a pretense, made up to fool people. Nothing is ever really owned.

## The Basic Reason

The basic reason the antisocial personality behaves as he or she does lies in a hidden terror of others.

To such a person every other being is an enemy, an enemy to be covertly or overtly destroyed.

The fixation is that survival itself depends on "keeping others down" or "keeping people ignorant."

If anyone were to promise to make others stronger or brighter, the antisocial personality suffers the utmost agony of personal danger.

They reason that if they are in this much trouble with people around them weak or stupid, they would perish should anyone become strong or bright.

Such a person has no trust to a point of terror. This is usually masked and unrevealed.

When such a personality goes insane, the world is full of Martians or the FBI and each person met is really a Martian or FBI agent.

But the bulk of such people exhibit no outward signs of insanity. They appear quite rational. They can be *very* convincing.

However, the list given above consists of things which such a personality cannot detect in himself or herself. This is so true that if you thought you found yourself in one of the above, you most certainly are not antisocial. Self-criticism is a luxury the antisocial cannot afford. They must be *right* because they are in continual danger in their own estimation. If you proved one *wrong*, you might even send him or her into a severe illness.

Only the sane, well-balanced person tries to correct his conduct.

## *Relief*

If you were to weed out of your past by proper search and discovery those antisocial persons you have known and if you then disconnected, you might experience great relief.

Similarly, if society were to recognize this personality type as a sick being as they now isolate people with smallpox, both social and economic recoveries could occur.

Things are not likely to get much better so long as 20 percent of the population is permitted to dominate and injure the lives and enterprise of the remaining 80 percent.

As majority rule is the political manner of the day, so should majority sanity express itself in our daily lives without the interference and destruction of the socially unwell.

The pity of it is, they will not permit themselves to be helped and would not respond to treatment if help were attempted.

An understanding and ability to recognize such personalities could bring a major change in society and our lives.

*The antisocial personality has a hidden terror of others.*

*All other people are enemies to be covertly or overtly destroyed.*

*One sign of an antisocial personality is that he deals mainly in critical or hostile remarks, invalidation and general suppression.*

DON'T FEEL TOO BAD. NOT EVERYONE IS BORN WITH TALENT.

# THE SOCIAL PERSONALITY

Man in his anxieties is prone to witch hunts.

All one has to do is designate "people wearing black caps" as the villains and one can start a slaughter of people in black caps.

This characteristic makes it very easy for the antisocial personality to bring about a chaotic or dangerous environment.

Man is not naturally brave or calm in his human state. And he is not necessarily villainous.

Even the antisocial personality, in his warped way, is quite certain that he is acting for the best and commonly sees himself as the only good person around, doing all for the good of everyone—the only flaw in his reasoning being that if one kills everyone else, none are left to be protected from the imagined evils. His *conduct* in his environment and toward his fellows is the only method of detecting either the antisocial or the social personalities. Their motives for self are similar—self-preservation and survival. They simply go about achieving these in different ways.

Thus, as man is naturally neither calm nor brave, anyone to some degree tends to be alert to dangerous persons and, hence, witch hunts can begin.

It is therefore even more important to identify the social personality than the antisocial personality. One then avoids shooting the innocent out of mere prejudice or dislike or because of some momentary misconduct.

The social personality can be defined most easily by comparison with his opposite, the antisocial personality.

This differentiation is easily done and no test should ever be constructed which isolates only the antisocial. On the same test must appear the upper as well as lower ranges of man's actions.

A test that declares only antisocial personalities without also being able to identify the social personality would be itself a suppressive test. It would be like answering "Yes" or "No" to the question "Do you still beat your wife?" Anyone who took it could be found guilty. While this mechanism might have suited the times of the Inquisition, it would not suit modern needs.

As the society runs, prospers and lives *solely* through the efforts of social personalities, one must know them as *they,* not the antisocial, are the worthwhile people. These are the people who must have rights and freedom. Attention is given to the antisocial solely to protect and assist the social personalities in the society.

All majority rules, civilizing intentions and even the human race will fail unless one can identify and thwart the antisocial personalities and help and forward the social personalities in the society. For the very word "society" implies social conduct and without it there is no society at all, only a barbarism with all men, good or bad, at risk.

The frailty of showing how the harmful people can be known is that these then apply the characteristics to decent people to get them hunted down and eradicated.

The swan song of every great civilization is the tune played by arrows, axes or bullets used by the antisocial to slay the last decent men.

Government is only dangerous when it can be employed by and for antisocial personalities. The end result is the eradication of all social personalities and the resultant collapse of Egypt, Babylon, Rome, Russia or the West.

You will note in the characteristics of the antisocial personality that intelligence is not a clue to the antisocial. They are bright or stupid or average. Thus, those who are extremely intelligent can rise to considerable, even head-of-state heights.

Importance and ability or wish to rise above others are likewise not indexes to the antisocial. When they do become important or rise, they are, however, rather visible by the broad consequences of their acts. But they are as likely to be unimportant people or hold very lowly stations and wish for nothing better.

Thus, it is the twelve given characteristics alone which identify the antisocial personality. And these same twelve reversed are the sole criteria of the social personality if one wishes to be truthful about them.

The identification or labeling of an antisocial personality cannot be done honestly and accurately unless one *also,* in the same examination of the person, reviews the positive side of his life.

All persons under stress can react with momentary flashes of antisocial conduct. This does not make them antisocial personalities.

The true antisocial person has a majority of antisocial characteristics.

The social personality has a majority of social characteristics.

Thus, one must examine the good with the bad before one can truly label the antisocial or the social.

In reviewing such matters, very broad testimony and evidence are best. One or two isolated instances determine nothing. One should search all twelve social and all twelve antisocial characteristics and decide on the basis of actual evidence, not opinion.

The twelve primary characteristics of the social personality are as follows:

**1. The social personality is specific in relating circumstances.** "Joe Jones said..." "*The Star* newspaper reported..." and gives sources of data where important or possible.

He may use the generality of "they" or "people" but seldom in connection with attributing statements or opinions of an alarming nature.

**2. The social personality is eager to relay good news and reluctant to relay bad.**

He may not even bother to pass along criticism when it doesn't matter.

He is more interested in making another feel liked or wanted than disliked by others and tends to err toward reassurance rather than toward criticism.

**3. A social personality passes communication without much alteration and if deleting anything tends to delete injurious matters.**

He does not like to hurt people's feelings. He sometimes errs in holding back bad news or orders which seem critical or harsh.

**4. Treatment and reform work very well on the social personality.**

Whereas antisocial people sometimes promise to reform, they do not. Only the social personality can change or improve easily.

It is often enough to point out unwanted conduct to a social personality to completely alter it for the better.

Criminal codes and violent punishment are not needed to regulate social personalities.

**5. The friends and associates of a social personality tend to be well, happy and of good morale.**

A truly social personality quite often produces betterment in health or fortune by his mere presence on the scene.

At the very least he does not reduce the existing levels of health or morale in his associates.

When ill, the social personality heals or recovers in an expected manner, and is found open to successful treatment.

**6. The social personality tends to select correct targets for correction.**

He fixes the tire that is flat rather than attack the windscreen.

In the mechanical arts he can therefore repair things and make them work.

**7. Cycles of action begun are ordinarily completed by the social personality, if possible.**

**8. The social personality is ashamed of his misdeeds and reluctant to confess them. He takes responsibility for his errors.**

**9. The social personality supports constructive groups and tends to protest or resist destructive groups.**

**10. Destructive actions are protested by the social personality. He assists constructive or helpful actions.**

**11. The social personality helps others and actively resists acts which harm others.**

**12. Property is property of someone to the social personality and its theft or misuse is prevented or frowned upon.**

## The Basic Motivation

The social personality naturally operates on the basis of the greatest good.

He is not haunted by imagined enemies but he does recognize real enemies when they exist.

The social personality wants to survive and wants others to survive, whereas the antisocial personality really and covertly wants others to succumb.

Basically, the social personality wants others to be happy and do well, whereas the antisocial personality is very clever in making others do very badly indeed.

A basic clue to the social personality is not really his successes but his motivations. The social personality when successful is often a target for the antisocial and by this reason he may fail. But his intentions included others in his success, whereas the antisocial only appreciate the doom of others.

Unless we can detect the social personality and hold him safe from undue restraint and detect also the antisocial and restrain him, our society will go on suffering from insanity, criminality and war, and man and civilization will not endure.

Of all our technical skills in Scientology, such differentiation ranks the highest since, failing, no other skill can continue, as the base on which it operates—civilization—will not be here to continue it.

Do not smash the social personality—and do not fail to render powerless the antisocial in their efforts to harm the rest of us.

Just because a man rises above his fellows or takes an important part does not make him an antisocial personality. Just because a man can control or dominate others does not make him an antisocial personality.

It is his motives in doing so and the consequences of his acts which distinguish the antisocial from the social.

Unless we realize and apply the true characteristics of the two types of personality, we will continue to live in a quandary of who our enemies are and, in doing so, victimize our friends.

All men have committed acts of violence or omission for which they could be censured. In all mankind there is not one single perfect human being.

But there are those who try to do right and those who specialize in wrong and upon these facts and characteristics you can know them.

*Social personalities are motivated by the desire to help others and do the greatest good for the greatest number. The bulk of humanity is composed of social personalities.*

# Basic Terms
# and Definitions

Often a social personality is so mired down in his own difficulties that he cannot *see* improvement is possible. To him, his setbacks and travails are "just life" or "the way things have to be." He has no inkling that such a thing as antisocial personalities exist or that one (or more) were making life miserable for him.

To become aware that such a condition exists requires one understand what the condition is. Following are basic terms and definitions associated with the detection and handling of antisocial personalities and those affected by them. These need to be understood for success in addressing and handling personal suppression.

*Suppressive Person:* (abbreviated "SP"). A person who seeks to *suppress,* or squash, any betterment activity or group. A suppressive person suppresses other people in his vicinity. This is the person whose behavior is calculated to be disastrous. "Suppressive person" or a "suppressive" is another name for the "antisocial personality."

*Potential Trouble Source:* (abbreviated "PTS"). A person who is in some way connected to and being adversely affected by a suppressive person. He is called a *potential* trouble source because he can be a lot of trouble to himself and to others.

An indicator of someone being a potential trouble source is *not* whether that person looks intimidated or not cheerful or is having trouble with his boss. Those are not things that indicate whether someone is a PTS. The indicators are very precise.

The PTS is connected to an SP who is antagonistic to him. The suppressive person keeps the potential trouble source from functioning in life. Therefore, the potential trouble source can do well in life or in some activity and then, when he meets up with or is affected by the suppressive person—who is somehow invalidating or making less of him or his efforts—he gets worse.

A potential trouble source is doing well and then not doing well, doing well, not doing well. When he is not doing well, he is sometimes ill.

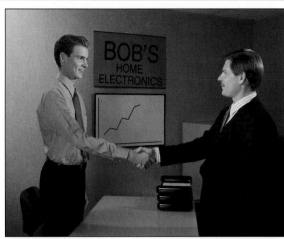

*A potential trouble source has periods in life when he does well.*

*But when he comes under the influence of a suppressive person . . .*

*. . . he begins doing poorly. He may become ill or have accidents and generally do worse in life.*

A person in this condition *roller-coasters*. The term *roller-coaster* means to better and worsen—the person gets better, gets worse, gets better, gets worse. Its name was derived from the name of an amusement park ride that rises then plunges steeply.

Another indicator of a potential trouble source is that in the presence of suppression, an individual makes mistakes. When a person makes mistakes or does stupid things, it is evidence that a suppressive person exists in that vicinity.

There are also types of PTS people. The basic ones are as follows.

## PTS Type I

The first type of PTS person is one who is associated with or connected to a suppressive person in his present time environment. By "connected to" is meant in the vicinity of, or in communication with in some way, whether a social, familial or business relationship.

*A Type I PTS has a suppressive person there in his present time environment trying to squash and invalidate him.*

An artist may have a "friend" hanging around who is actually a suppressive person, invalidating his work and ambitions. The artist may become ill or give up his work.

An executive with a suppressive person for a business associate will roller-coaster and may find himself making mistakes in his work, suffering setbacks or becoming sick.

Also, an individual may be involved in betterment activities to increase his abilities and improve his life and the lives of others. Such an individual may be connected to a suppressive person. The SP attacks such betterment activities and the people involved in them, as the suppressive is terrified of anyone becoming stronger or more able.

Thus individuals intimately connected with persons (such as marital or familial ties) of known antagonism to betterment activities are PTS. In practice, these persons have such pressure continually brought to bear upon them by others with undue influence over them, they make poor progress or improvement, and their interest is solely devoted to proving the antagonistic element wrong.

*Someone intimately connected to another who opposes their attempts at self-betterment is PTS.*

## PTS Type II

In the second type of PTS, a *past* suppression is being restimulated by someone or something in the present time environment. When an individual is restimulated, a past bad memory is reactivated due to similar circumstances existing in the present which approximate circumstances of the past, and the person can experience the pain and emotions contained in the past memory. In the case of a PTS Type II, the person wouldn't even have to see the suppressive person to go PTS but can become so just by seeing something that reminds him of the suppressive.

*A Type II PTS is reminded of a suppressive person in his past by someone or something in his environment. The actual suppressive is not there in present time but his influence is felt nevertheless.*

For example, if someone has been suppressed by a postman and sees a letter box when the postman isn't even around, that could be enough to cause him to roller-coaster.

A PTS Type II always has an *apparent* suppressive who is not *the* suppressive of the PTS person and is confusing the two and is acting PTS only because of restimulation, not because of suppression.

An important thing to know is that *a suppressive is always a person, a being or a group of beings.* A suppressive is *not* a condition, a problem or a conclusion, decision or resolution made by the individual himself.

The Type II PTS is handled by specific Scientology processes. These are exact sets of questions asked or directions given by a trained Scientology practitioner to help a person find out things about himself and improve his condition. Scientology processes received by a Type II PTS help the person locate the suppressive and fully alleviate the undue influences the SP has had on the PTS.

## PTS Type III

In this case the Type II's *apparent* SP (suppressive person) is spread all over the world and is often more than all the people there are—for the person sometimes has ghosts about him or demons and they are just more apparent SPs but imaginary as beings as well.

The Type III PTS is mostly found in mental institutions. He is best helped by providing a safe environment and giving him rest and quiet, and no treatment of a mental nature at all. He should receive any medical care needed that is unbrutal in nature.

*A Type III PTS is also under the influence of a suppressive from his past, but the present time environment is, to him, full of suppressives.*

A person who is PTS is often the last person to suspect it. He may have become temporarily or momentarily so. And he may have become so very slightly. Or he may be *very* PTS and have been so for a long time. Therefore, the very first step in handling this condition is to gain an understanding of the fundamentals of the technology concerning potential trouble sources and suppressive persons so that the situation can be handled.

And it *can* be handled.

# PTS Handling

There are two stable data which anyone has to have, understand and *know are true* in order to obtain results in handling the person connected to suppressives.

These data are:

1. That all illness in greater or lesser degree and all foul-ups stem directly and only from a PTS condition.

2. That getting rid of the condition requires three basic actions: (A) Discover; (B) Handle or (C) Disconnect.

Persons called upon to handle PTS people can do so very easily, far more easily than they believe. Their basic stumbling block is thinking that there are exceptions or that there is other technology or that the two above data have modifiers or are not sweeping. The moment a person who is trying to handle PTSes gets persuaded there are other conditions or reasons or technology, he is at once lost and will lose the game and not obtain results. And this is very too bad because it is not difficult and the results are there to be obtained.

A PTS person is rarely psychotic. But all psychotics are PTS if only to themselves. A PTS person may be in a state of deficiency or pathology (an unhealthy condition caused by a disease) which prevents a ready recovery, but at the same time he will not fully recover unless the PTS condition is also handled. For he became prone to deficiency or pathological illness because he was PTS. And unless the condition is relieved, no matter what medication or nutrition he may be given, he might not recover and certainly will not recover permanently. This seems to indicate that there are "other illnesses or reasons for illness besides being PTS." To be sure, there are deficiencies and illnesses just as there are accidents and injuries. But strangely enough, the person himself precipitates them (causes them to happen) because being PTS predisposes him (makes him susceptible) to them.

In a more garbled way, the medicos and nutritionists are always talking about "stress" causing illness. Lacking full technology on the subject as contained in Scientology, they yet have an inkling that this is so because they see it is somehow true. They cannot handle it. Yet they recognize it, and they state that it is a senior situation to various illnesses and accidents. Well, Scientology has the technology of this in more ways than one.

What is this thing called "stress"? It is more than the medico defines it—he usually says it comes from operational or physical shock and in this he has too limited a view.

A person under stress is actually under a suppression in one or more areas or aspects of his life.

If that suppression is located and the person handles or disconnects, the condition diminishes. If he also receives Scientology processes which address suppression of the individual and if *all* such areas of suppression are thus handled, the person would recover from anything caused by "stress."

Usually, the person has insufficient understanding of life or any area of it to grasp his own situation. He is confused. He believes all his illnesses are true because they occur in such heavy books!

At some time he was predisposed to illness or accidents. When a serious suppression then occurred, he suffered a precipitation or occurrence of the accident or illness, and then with a series of repeated similar suppressions, the illness or tendency to accidents became prolonged or chronic.

To say then that a person is PTS to his current environment would be very limited as a diagnosis. If he continues to do or be something to which the suppressive person or group objected, he may become or continue to be ill or have accidents.

Actually, the problem of PTS is not very complicated. Once you have grasped the two data first given, the rest of it becomes simply an analysis of how they apply to this particular person.

A PTS person can be markedly helped in three ways:

a. Gaining an understanding of the technology of the condition

b. Discovering to what or to whom he is PTS

c. Handling or disconnecting

Someone with the wish or duty to find and handle PTSes has an additional prior step: he must know how to recognize a PTS and how to handle them when recognized. Thus, it is rather a waste of time to engage in this hunt unless one has thoroughly studied the material on suppressives and PTSes and grasps it without misunderstanding the words or terms used. In other words, the first step of the person is to get a grasp of the subject and its technology. This is not difficult to do.

With this step done, a person has no real trouble recognizing PTS people and can have success in handling them which is very gratifying and rewarding.

Let us consider the easiest level of approach:

i. Give the person the simpler materials on the subject and let him study them so that he knows the elements like "PTS" and "suppressive." He may just come to realize the source of his difficulties right there and be much better. It has happened.

ii. Have him discuss the illness or accident or condition, without much prodding or probing, that he thinks now may be the result of suppression. He will usually tell you it is right here and now or was a short time ago and will be all set to explain it (without any relief) as stemming from his current environment or a recent one. If you let it go at that, he would simply be a bit unhappy and not get well as he is discussing usually a recent disturbing experience that has a lot of earlier similar experiences below it.

iii. Ask when he recalls first having that illness or having such accidents. He will at once begin to roll this back and realize that it has happened before. He will get back to some early this-lifetime point usually.

iv. Now ask him *who* it was. He will usually tell you promptly. And, as you are not trying to do more than release him from the restimulation that occurred, you don't probe any further.

v. You will usually find that he has named a person to whom he is still connected! So you ask him whether he wants to handle or disconnect. Now, as the sparks will really fly in his life if he dramatically disconnects and if he can't see how he can, you persuade him to begin to handle with a gradual approach. This may consist of imposing some slight discipline on him, such as requiring him to actually answer his mail or write the person a pleasant good roads, good weather (calm, warm, friendly) note or to realistically look at how he turned them from being affectionate to being indifferent, disliking or hateful. In short, what is required in the handling is an easy, gradual approach. All you are trying to do is MOVE THE PTS PERSON FROM BEING THE EFFECT OF SUPPRESSION OVER TO BEING IN A POSITION OF SLIGHT GENTLE CAUSE OVER IT.

vi. Check with the person again, if he is handling, and coach him along, always at a gentle good-roads-and-good-weather level.

That is a simple handling. You can get complexities such as a person being PTS to an unknown person in his immediate vicinity that he may have to find before he can handle or disconnect. You can find people who can't remember more than a few years back. But simple handling ends when it looks pretty complex. When you run into such

*To handle PTSness it is first necessary to understand its mechanics.*

*Get the person to discuss the illness or accident or condition she feels may be the result of suppression.*

*The person is asked when she first recalls having such accidents, and her attention will go to an earlier one.*

*By asking who it was, the person will usually tell you promptly...*

*... and, having spotted the source, can then begin to improve.*

complexity, it can be handled by more advanced procedures in Scientology.

But this simple handling will get you quite a few stars in your crown. You will be amazed to find that while some of them don't instantly recover, medication, vitamins, minerals will now work when before they wouldn't. You may also get some instant recoveries but realize that if they don't, you have not failed.

By doing the PTS handling steps laid out in this section, you have made an entrance and you have stirred things up and gotten the PTS person more aware and just that way you will find he is in a more causative position.

His illness or proneness to accidents may not be slight. You may succeed only to the point where he now has a chance, by nutrition, vitamins, minerals, medication, treatment, and above all, Scientology processing, of getting well. Unless you jogged this condition, he had no chance at all: for becoming PTS is the first thing that happened to him on the subject of illness or accidents.

So do not underestimate what you can do for a PTS. And don't sell PTS technology short or neglect it. And don't push off, or even worse tolerate, PTS conditions in people.

You *can* do something about it.

And so can they.

# FURTHER DATA
# ON PTS HANDLING

A person applying PTS technology to his own life or to another who is roller-coasting can encounter a unique circumstance. The PTS person correctly carries out the standard action to handle a person who is antagonistic to him or his activities, yet the antagonistic source continues to remain antipathetic to the PTS person and/or his activities. In this case, it may require the alternate step to *handle*, which is *disconnect*.

The concept of disconnection relates to the right to communicate.

Perhaps the most fundamental right of any being is the right to communicate. Without this freedom, other rights deteriorate.

Communication, however, is a two-way flow. If one has the right to communicate, then one must also have the right to not receive communication from another. It is this latter concept of the right to not receive communication that gives us our right to privacy.

These rights are so basic that governments have written them into laws—witness the American Bill of Rights.

However, groups have always regulated these rights to one degree or another. For with the freedom to communicate come certain agreements and responsibilities.

An example of this is a marriage: In a monogamous society, the agreement is that one will be married to only one person at one time. That agreement extends to having sexual relations with one's spouse and no one else. Thus, should wife Shirley establish this type of relationship with someone other than her husband Pete, it is a violation of the agreement and resolutions of the marriage. Pete has the right to insist that either this communication cease or that the marriage will cease.

# Handle or Disconnect

In this booklet, you have seen the phrase "handle or disconnect." It means simply that.

The term *handle* most commonly means, when used in relation to PTS technology, to smooth out a situation with another person by applying the technology of communication.

The term *disconnection* is defined as a self-determined decision made by an individual that he is not going to be connected to another. It is a severing of a communication line (the route along which a communication travels from one person to another).

The basic principle of handle or disconnect exists in any group.

It is much like trying to deal with a criminal. If he will not handle, the society resorts to the only other solution: It "disconnects" the criminal from the society. In other words, they remove the guy from society and put him in a prison because he won't *handle* his problem or otherwise cease to commit criminal acts against others.

It's the same sort of situation that husband Pete is faced with as mentioned in the first part of this section. The optimum solution is to handle the situation with wife Shirley and her violations of their group (marriage) agreements. But if Pete cannot handle the situation, he is left with no other choice but to disconnect (sever the marriage communication lines if only by separation). To do otherwise would be disastrous, for he is connected to someone antagonistic to the original agreements, decisions, resolutions and responsibilities of the group (the marriage).

A person can become PTS by reason of being connected to someone that is antagonistic to him. In order to resolve the PTS condition, he either *handles* the other person's antagonism (as covered in the materials in this booklet) or, as a last resort when all attempts to handle have failed, he disconnects from the person. He is simply exercising his right to communicate or not to communicate with a particular person.

By applying the technology of handle or disconnect, the person is, in actual fact, doing nothing different than any society or group or marriage down through thousands of years.

**The Right to Disconnect**

Earlier, the use of disconnection in Scientology had been cancelled. It had been abused by a few individuals who'd failed to handle situations which could have been handled and who lazily or senselessly disconnected, thereby creating situations even worse than the original because it was the wrong action.

Secondly, there were those who could survive only by living on Scientology's lines—they wanted to continue to be connected to Scientologists. Thus, they screamed to high heaven if anyone dared to apply the tech of "handle or disconnect."

This put Scientologists at a disadvantage.

We cannot afford to deny Scientologists that basic freedom that is granted to everyone else: the right to choose whom one wishes to communicate with or not communicate with. It's bad enough that there are governments trying, through the use of force, to prevent people from disconnecting from them.

The bare fact is that disconnection is a vital tool in handling PTSness and can be very effective when used correctly.

Therefore the tool of disconnection was restored to use, in the hands of those persons thoroughly and standardly trained in the technology of handling suppressives and potential trouble sources.

**Handling Antagonistic Sources**

In the great majority of cases, where a person has some family member or close associate who appears antagonistic to him, it is *not* really a matter of the antagonistic source wanting the PTS to not *get better.* It can more commonly be a lack of correct information about what the PTS person is doing that causes the problem or upset. In such a case, simply having the PTS disconnect would not help matters and would actually show an inability on the part of the PTS to confront the situation. It is quite common that the PTS has a low confront (ability to face without flinching or avoiding) on the person and situation. This isn't hard to understand when one looks at these facts:

a. To be PTS in the first place, the PTS must have committed harmful, contrasurvival acts against the antagonistic source; and

b. When one has committed such acts, his confront and responsibility drop.

When an individual using the data in this booklet to assist another finds that the person is PTS to a family member, he does *not* recommend that the person disconnect from the antagonistic source. The advice to the PTS person is to *handle*.

The handling for such a situation is to educate the PTS person in the technology of PTSness and suppression, and then skillfully and firmly guide the PTS through the steps needed to restore good communication with the antagonistic source. For example, where the PTS person is a Scientologist, these actions eventually dissolve the situation by bringing about an *understanding* on the part of the antagonistic source as to what Scientology is and why the PTS person is interested and involved in it.

## When Disconnection Is Used

One can encounter a situation where someone is factually connected to a suppressive person, in present time. This is a person whose normal operating basis is one of making others smaller, less able, less powerful. He does not want anyone to get better, at all.

In truth, an SP is absolutely, completely terrified of anyone becoming more powerful.

In such an instance the PTS isn't going to get anywhere trying to "handle" the person. The answer is to sever the connection.

How a disconnection is done depends on the circumstances.

*Example:* The person lives next door to, say, a psychiatric clinic and feels PTS due to this environment. The remedy is simple—the person can move to another apartment in another location. He need not write any sort of "disconnection letter" to the psychiatric clinic. He simply changes his environment—which is, in effect, a disconnection from the suppressive environment.

*Example:* One discovers that an employee at his place of business is an SP—he steals money, drives away customers, wipes out other employees and will not correct no matter what you do. The handling is very simple—the PTS fires him and that's the end of it right there!

The individual's right to communicate (or not) with someone is an inherent freedom. Exercising this right and disconnecting from a suppressive person does not under any circumstances justify any violations of the laws of the land.

The technology of disconnection is essential in the handling of PTSes. It can and has saved lives and untold trouble and upset. It must be preserved and used correctly.

# EASE OF HANDLING

In handling the PTS person, the main emphasis has to be on properly doing the steps necessary to handle. If he does so, he will begin to get well, cease to have problems and no longer roller-coaster. One must realize the simplicity of handling the PTS person: it requires no heroic or drastic actions and is done on a very, very gradual approach. It doesn't have to be an explosive handling; it can be very gentle. Handling a PTS condition with a step-by-step approach frees the PTS from the restraints holding him back, brings the person up to a causative position and enables him to achieve a productive and rewarding life.

Detection of antisocial personalities or suppressive persons not only brings relief to the individuals they affect, but recognition of these personalities and an understanding of the havoc they wreak would truly benefit all society. Likewise, knowing the traits of social personalities enables one to wisely choose those individuals for his friends and associates. With this knowledge and its application in everyday life, man can create a sane community and civilization for himself, his family and his fellows. ■

# Practical Exercises

*These exercises will help you identify and handle suppression. By doing them, your understanding of the subject will increase.*

1 Look around your environment and find an example of antisocial behavior in another. Note which antisocial attribute is being demonstrated by the person. Repeat the above nine more times.

2 Look around your environment and find an example of social behavior in another. Note which social attribute is being demonstrated by the person. Repeat the above nine more times.

3 Think of an antisocial characteristic in someone you have known or observed. Then think of a social characteristic in that person or someone else you have known or observed. Do this again and again, spotting examples of antisocial or social characteristics in different people you have known or observed. Keep this up until you feel confident in your ability to recognize antisocial characteristics or social characteristics in people.

4 Find a friend, relative or associate who is ill or roller-coastering. Do a PTS handling on this person, beginning with educating the person on PTSness and continuing all the way through the complete handling: your actions are to include checking with the person again and coaching him along at a good-roads-and-good-weather level until he has moved from being the effect of the suppression to a position of slight, gentle cause over it.

# RESULTS FROM APPLICATION

**K**nowing what causes the precipitation of illnesses and the exact reason why some people do well in life for a time and then do poorly has made a tremendous difference in many lives.

People using the discoveries of L. Ron Hubbard do not resort to drugs to relieve stress and anxiety and don't have to mask symptoms with medications. The apathetic advice that one has to learn to live with his condition surrenders to effective action. Illnesses, injuries and goofs of every type are *caused*—and not by an imbalance of chemicals in the brain. Purely physical approaches to resolve nonoptimum conditions which do not involve the individual himself always fall short. More than 80 percent of those who apply Mr. Hubbard's technology on the handling of suppression miss almost no time from work due to illness. None take street drugs. The following are testimonials to the fact that life can be lived free of suppression, illnesses and accidents.

**H**aving spent years trying to handle a physical problem, a legal secretary from St. Louis was finally rescued by a friend who advised him to study Mr. Hubbard's data regarding illness and suppression.

*"Boy, what a **relief!** I have literally spent thousands of dollars trying to figure out what was going on with my kidney. Well, I now know what kind of effect a person can have on his body when he's in an environment that's holding him down or if he is connected to a person who's constantly telling him how he's not worth much to himself or others. By finding out about this technology I was able to really open my eyes to the fact that I've been living with someone who's been the ruin of my life for years. I was not able to see this before because I was right in the middle of a tornado, you could say, and had become part of that confusion. It's such a relief to no longer feel like I'm on a roller coaster, feeling happy one moment and completely desperate the next. And don't think that you can get bored feeling 'up' most of the time—believe me, it is much more fun than riding a roller coaster that's totally out of control and being monitored by another!"*

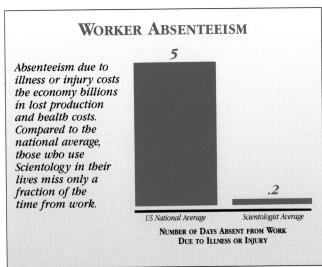

## WORKER ABSENTEEISM

*Absenteeism due to illness or injury costs the economy billions in lost production and health costs. Compared to the national average, those who use Scientology in their lives miss only a fraction of the time from work.*

5

.2

US National Average      Scientologist Average

**NUMBER OF DAYS ABSENT FROM WORK DUE TO ILLNESS OR INJURY**

A California woman had lost her husband. Although she had been a cheerful person previously, she was now having difficulties in her life and relationships. She wanted another husband and a family, but hadn't been able to achieve this. Instead, she dedicated most of her life to the company she was working for. However, the situation reached the point where she hated her work and had been ill and absent from the job for weeks. Life was passing her by; she had become so depressed that she had considered seeing a psychiatrist. Her sister was concerned when she heard this and decided to apply the technology of handling suppression before the psychiatrist got to her.

*"After going through the material about the antisocial personality, my sister realized that the manager of the company where she worked was a suppressive person and was not only the cause of her immediate problems, but also the cause of her late husband's illnesses and problems in life. She saw how the manager had used her and her husband for his own personal gains and was now invalidating her. He had also, with his own unethical behavior, nearly destroyed another couple's marriage.*

*"My sister was amazed at the relief she experienced when she realized this; she immediately became cause over the situation, talked to the manager and told him exactly what she saw he was doing. She quit the job.*

*"Shortly after this, I received a letter from my sister saying that she had new friends and a new job and was overjoyed to tell me that she was getting married. Five years later she has a family and is happy and doing very well in life."*

The remarriage of her father spelled misfortune for a young girl from Nevada, as she could not get along with her new stepmother. As the years went by, this deteriorated to the point where the girl felt there was no hope for their relationship; she left home at the age of eighteen after a vicious fight with her stepmother. This was upsetting to the rest of the family as the girl and her father had been very close. Some time later she learned about Mr. Hubbard's discoveries on suppressive persons and, using this technology, handled the situation.

*"My stepmother had been an alcoholic and had been under treatment by psychologists and psychiatrists for years, trying to handle this condition. Their 'handling' was to give her drugs and tell her what to think and do in life. As a result, her outlook on life had been bleak and very negative. I finally discovered the technology about suppressive persons. I found out who had been suppressing my stepmother and I learned how to help her. Today she doesn't go to psychiatrists anymore, doesn't drink at all, is completely cheerful—we get along great! After all these years, I am **extremely** proud that we have a happy family."*

# GLOSSARY

**aberrated:** affected by *aberration*, a departure from rational thought or behavior. Aberration means basically to err, to make mistakes, or more specifically to have fixed ideas which are not true. The word is also used in its scientific sense. It means departure from a straight line. If a line should go from A to B, then if it is *aberrated* it would go from A to some other point, to some other point, to some other point, to some other point, to some other point, and finally arrive at B. Taken in its scientific sense, it would also mean the lack of straightness or to see crookedly as, for example, a man sees a horse but thinks he sees an elephant. Aberrated conduct would be wrong conduct, or conduct not supported by reason. Aberration is opposed to sanity, which would be its opposite. From the Latin, *aberrare*, to wander from; Latin, *ab*, away, *errare*, to wander.

**communication line:** the route along which a communication travels from one person to another.

**confront:** to face without flinching or avoiding. The ability to confront is actually the ability to be there comfortably and perceive.

**cycle of action:** the sequence that an action goes through, wherein the action is begun, is continued for as long as is required and then is completed as planned.

**invalidation:** refuting, degrading, discrediting or denying something someone else considers to be fact.

**potential trouble source:** a person who is in some way connected to and being adversely affected by a suppressive person. He is called a *potential* trouble source because he can be a lot of trouble to himself and to others.

**present time:** the time which is now and becomes the past as rapidly as it is observed. It is a term loosely applied to the environment existing in now.

**process:** an exact series of directions or sequence of actions taken to accomplish a desired result.

**processing:** a special form of personal counseling, unique in Scientology, which helps an individual look at his own existence and improves his ability to confront what he is and where he is. Processing is a precise, thoroughly codified activity with exact procedures.

**PTS:** abbreviation for *potential trouble source*. *See* **potential trouble source** in this glossary.

**restimulated:** affected by *restimulation*, the reactivation of a memory of a past unpleasant experience due to similar circumstances in the present approximating circumstances of the past. When a person is restimulated, he can experience the pain and emotions contained in the past memory.

**roller-coaster:** to better and worsen—a person gets better, gets worse, gets better, gets worse. The term was derived from the name of an amusement park ride that rises and then plunges steeply.

**Scientology:** an applied religious philosophy developed by L. Ron Hubbard. It is the study and handling of the spirit in relationship to itself, universes and other life. The word *Scientology* comes from the Latin *scio,* which means "know" and the Greek word *logos,* meaning "the word or outward form by which the inward thought is expressed and made known." Thus, Scientology means knowing about knowing.

**SP:** abbreviation for *suppressive person*. *See* **suppressive person** in this glossary.

**suppressive person:** a person who possesses a distinct set of characteristics and mental attitudes that cause him to suppress other people in his vicinity. This is the person whose behavior is calculated to be disastrous. Also called *antisocial personality.*

# ABOUT L. RON HUBBARD

Born in Tilden, Nebraska on March 13, 1911, his road of discovery and dedication to his fellows began at an early age. By the age of nineteen, he had traveled more than a quarter of a million miles, examining the cultures of Java, Japan, India and the Philippines.

Returning to the United States in 1929, Ron resumed his formal education and studied mathematics, engineering and the then new field of nuclear physics—all providing vital tools for continued research. To finance that research, Ron embarked upon a literary career in the early 1930s, and soon became one of the most widely read authors of popular fiction. Yet never losing sight of his primary goal, he continued his mainline research through extensive travel and expeditions.

With the advent of World War II, he entered the United States Navy as a lieutenant (junior grade) and served as commander of antisubmarine corvettes. Left partially blind and lame from injuries sustained during combat, he was diagnosed as permanently disabled by 1945. Through application of his theories on the mind, however, he was not only able to help fellow servicemen, but also to regain his own health.

After five more years of intensive research, Ron's discoveries were presented to the world in *Dianetics: The Modern Science of Mental Health*. The first popular handbook on the human mind expressly written for the man in the street, *Dianetics* ushered in a new era of hope for mankind and a new phase of life for its author. He did, however, not cease his research, and as breakthrough after breakthrough was carefully codified through late 1951, the applied religious philosophy of Scientology was born.

Because Scientology explains the whole of life, there is no aspect of man's existence that L. Ron Hubbard's subsequent work did not address. Residing variously in the United States and England, his continued research brought forth solutions to such social ills as declining educational standards and pandemic drug abuse.

All told, L. Ron Hubbard's works on Scientology and Dianetics total forty million words of recorded lectures, books and writings. Together, these constitute the legacy of a lifetime that ended on January 24, 1986. Yet the passing of L. Ron Hubbard in no way constituted an end; for with a hundred million of his books in circulation and millions of people daily applying his technologies for betterment, it can truly be said the world still has no greater friend. ■

# CHURCHES OF SCIENTOLOGY

## WESTERN UNITED STATES

**Church of Scientology of Arizona**
2111 W. University Dr.
Mesa, Arizona 85201

**Church of Scientology of the Valley**
15643 Sherman Way
Van Nuys, California 91406

**Church of Scientology of Los Angeles**
4810 Sunset Boulevard
Los Angeles, California 90027

**Church of Scientology of Los Gatos**
475 Alberto Way, Suite 110
Los Gatos, California 95032

**Church of Scientology of Mountain View**
2483 Old Middlefield Way
Mountain View, California 96043

**Church of Scientology of Pasadena**
1277 East Colorado Boulevard
Pasadena, California 91106

**Church of Scientology of Sacramento**
825 15th Street
Sacramento, California 95814

**Church of Scientology of San Diego**
1330 4th Avenue
San Diego, California 92101

**Church of Scientology of San Francisco**
83 McAllister Street
San Francisco, California 94102

**Church of Scientology of Stevens Creek**
80 E. Rosemary
San Jose, California 95112

**Church of Scientology of Santa Barbara**
524 State Street
Santa Barbara, California 93101

**Church of Scientology of Orange County**
1451 Irvine Boulevard
Tustin, California 92680

**Church of Scientology of Colorado**
3385 S. Bannock
Englewood, Colorado 80110

**Church of Scientology of Hawaii**
1148 Bethel Street
Honolulu, Hawaii 96813

**Church of Scientology of Minnesota**
Twin Cities
1011 Nicollet Mall
Minneapolis, Minnesota 55403

**Church of Scientology of Kansas City**
3619 Broadway
Kansas City, Missouri 64111

**Church of Scientology of Missouri**
9510 Page Boulevard
St. Louis, Missouri 63132

**Church of Scientology of Nevada**
846 E. Sahara Avenue
Las Vegas, Nevada 89104

**Church of Scientology of New Mexico**
8106 Menaul Boulevard N.E.
Albuquerque, New Mexico 87110

**Church of Scientology of Portland**
323 S.W. Washington
Portland, Oregon 97204

**Church of Scientology of Texas**
2200 Guadalupe
Austin, Texas 78705

**Church of Scientology of Utah**
1931 S. 1100 East
Salt Lake City, Utah 84106

**Church of Scientology of Washington State**
2226 3rd Avenue
Seattle, Washington 98121

## EASTERN UNITED STATES

**Church of Scientology of Connecticut**
909 Whalley Avenue
New Haven, Connecticut 06515

**Church of Scientology of Florida**
120 Giralda Avenue
Coral Gables, Florida 33134

**Church of Scientology of Orlando**
1830 East Colonial Drive
Orlando, Florida 32803

**Church of Scientology of Tampa**
3617 Henderson Boulevard
Tampa, Florida 33609

**Church of Scientology of Georgia**
1132 West Peachtree Street
Atlanta, Georgia 30309

**Church of Scientology of Illinois**
3009 North Lincoln Avenue
Chicago, Illinois 60657

**Church of Scientology of Boston**
448 Beacon Street
Boston, Massachusetts 02115

**Church of Scientology of Ann Arbor**
2355 West Stadium Boulevard
Ann Arbor, Michigan 48103

**Church of Scientology of Michigan**
321 Williams Street
Royal Oak, Michigan 48067

**Church of Scientology of Buffalo**
47 West Huron Street
Buffalo, New York 14202

**Church of Scientology of Long Island**
99 Railroad Station Plaza
Hicksville, New York 11801

**Church of Scientology of New York**
227 West 46th Street
New York City, New York 10036

**Church of Scientology of Cincinnati**
215 West 4th Street, 5th Floor
Cincinnati, Ohio 45202

**Church of Scientology of Ohio**
30 North High Street
Columbus, Ohio 43215

**Church of Scientology of Pennsylvania**
1315 Race Street
Philadelphia, Pennsylvania 19107

**Founding Church of Scientology of Washington, DC**
1701 20th Street N.W.
Washington, DC 20009

## PUERTO RICO

**Church of Scientology of Puerto Rico**
272 JT Piniero Avenue
Hyde Park, Hato Rey
Puerto Rico 00918

## UNITED KINGDOM

**Church of Scientology of Birmingham**
Albert House, 3rd Floor
24 Albert Street
Birmingham
England B4 7UD

**Church of Scientology of Brighton**
5 St. Georges Place
London Road
Brighton, Sussex
England BN1 4GA

**Church of Scientology Saint Hill Foundation**
Saint Hill Manor
East Grinstead, West Sussex
England RH19 4JY

**Church of Scientology of London**
68 Tottenham Court Road
London
England W1P 0BB

**Church of Scientology of Manchester**
258 Deansgate
Manchester
England M3 4BG

**Church of Scientology of Plymouth**
41 Ebrington Street
Plymouth, Devon
England PL4 9AA

**Church of Scientology of Sunderland**
51 Fawcett Street
Sunderland, Tyne and Wear
England SR1 1RS

**Hubbard Academy of Personal Independence**
20 Southbridge
Edinburgh
Scotland EH1 1LL

## EUROPE

### Austria

**Church of Scientology of Austria**
Schottenfeldgasse 13/15
1070 Wien

### Belgium

**Church of Scientology of Belgium**
61, rue du Prince Royal
1050 Bruxelles

### Denmark

**Church of Scientology of Jylland**
Vester Alle 26
8000 Aarhus C

**Church of Scientology of Copenhagen**
Store Kongensgade 55
1264 Copenhagen K

**Church of Scientology of Denmark**
Gammel Kongevej 3–5, 1
1610 Copenhagen V

### France

**Church of Scientology of Angers**
21, rue Paul Bert
49100 Angers

**Church of Scientology of Clermont-Ferrand**
6, rue Dulaure
63000 Clermont-Ferrand

**Church of Scientology of Lyon**
3, place des Capucins
69001 Lyon

**Church of Scientology of Paris**
7, rue Jules César
75012 Paris, France

h of Scientology of
t-Étienne
e Marengo
 Saint-Étienne

## many
h of Scientology of Berlin
olzstraße 51–52
 Berlin
h of Scientology of
seldorf
ichstraße 28
 Düsseldorf
h of Scientology of
endorfer
dorfer Landstraße 35
 Hamburg, Germany
h of Scientology of Frankfurt
städter Landstraße 213
 Frankfurt
h of Scientology of Hamburg
amm 63
 Hamburg
h of Scientology of Hanover
tusstraße 2
 Hannover
h of Scientology of Munich
traße 12
 München
h of Scientology of Stuttgart
heimerstr. 9
 Stuttgart, Germany

## el
tics and Scientology
ege of Israel
ntzion
v 61573, Israel

## y
h of Scientology of Brescia
atelli Bronzetti, 20
 Brescia
h of Scientology of Catania
ribaldi, 9
 Catania
h of Scientology of Milan
etone, 10
 Milano
h of Scientology of Monza
ova Valassina, 354
 Lissone, MI
h of Scientology of Novara
ssalacqua, 28
 Novara
h of Scientology of Nuoro
marmora, 102
 Nuoro
h of Scientology of Padua
meli, 1/5
 Padova
h of Scientology of
denone
ntereale, 10/C
 Pordenone
h of Scientology of Rome
nnio N. 64
. Giovanni-Roma
 Roma

## Church of Scientology of Turin
Via Bersezio, 7
10152 Torino

## Church of Scientology of Verona
Corso Milano, 84
37138 Verona

# Netherlands
### Church of Scientology of Amsterdam
Nieuwe Zijds Voorburgwal 271
1012 RL Amsterdam

# Norway
### Church of Scientology of Norway
Lille Grensen 3
0159 Oslo 1

# Portugal
### Instituto de Dianética
Rua de Conde Redondo #19
1150 Lisboa, Portugal

# Russia
### Hubbard Humanitarian Center
Prospect Budyonogo 31
105275 Moscow

# Spain
### Dianetics Civil Association of
Barcelona
C/ Pau Clarís 85, Principal dcha.
08010 Barcelona

### Dianetics Civil Association of
Madrid
C/ Montera 20, Piso 1° dcha.
28013 Madrid

# Sweden
### Church of Scientology of Göteborg
Odinsgatan 8, 2 tr.
411 03 Göteborg

### Church of Scientology of Malmö
Porslingsgatan 3
211 32 Malmö

### Church of Scientology of Stockholm
Götgatan 105
116 62 Stockholm

# Switzerland
### Church of Scientology of Basel
Herrengrabenweg 56
4054 Basel

### Church of Scientology of Bern
Muhlemattstr. 31
Postfach 384
3000 Bern 14

### Church of Scientology of Geneva
Route de Saint-Julien 7–9 C.P. 823
1227 Carouge, Genève

### Church of Scientology of Lausanne
10, rue de la Madeleine
1003 Lausanne

### Church of Scientology of Zurich
Badenerstrasse 141
8004 Zürich

# AFRICA
### Church of Scientology of
Cape Town
St. Georges Centre, 2nd Floor
13 Hout Street
Cape Town 8001
Republic of South Africa

### Church of Scientology of Durban
57 College Lane
Durban 4001
Republic of South Africa

### Church of Scientology of
Johannesburg
6th Floor, Budget House
130 Main Street
Johannesburg 2001
Republic of South Africa

### Church of Scientology of
Johannesburg North
1st Floor Bordeaux Centre
Gordon and Jan Smuts Ave.
Blairgowrie, Randburg 2125
Republic of South Africa

### Church of Scientology of
Port Elizabeth
2 St. Christopher Place
27 Westbourne Road Central
Port Elizabeth 6001
Republic of South Africa

### Church of Scientology of Pretoria
306 Ancore Building
Jeppe and Esselen Streets
Pretoria 0002
Republic of South Africa

### Church of Scientology of Bulawayo
Southampton House, Suite 202
Main Street and 9th Avenue
Bulawayo
Zimbabwe

### Church of Scientology of Harare
PO Box 3524
87 Livingston Road
Harare
Zimbabwe

# AUSTRALIA, NEW ZEALAND AND OCEANIA
## Australia
### Church of Scientology of Adelaide
24–28 Waymouth Street
Adelaide, South Australia 5000

### Church of Scientology of Brisbane
106 Edward Street
Brisbane, Queensland 4000

### Church of Scientology of
Australian Capital Territory
43–45 East Row
Canberra City, ACT 2601

### Church of Scientology of
Melbourne
42–44 Russell Street
Melbourne, Victoria 3000

### Church of Scientology of Perth
108 Murray Street
Perth, Western Australia 6000

### Church of Scientology of Sydney
201 Castlereagh Street
Sydney, New South Wales 2000

## Japan
### Scientology Tokyo
1-23-1 Higashi Gotanda
Shinagawa-ku
Tokyo, Japan 141

## New Zealand
### Church of Scientology
New Zealand
159 Queen Street
Auckland 1

# LATIN AMERICA
## Argentina
### Dianetics Association of Argentina
1769 Santa Fe Avenue
Buenos Aires

## Colombia
### Dianetics Cultural Center
Carrera 30 #91–96
Santa Fé de Bogotá,
Bogotá

## Mexico
### Dianetics Cultural
Organization, A.C.
Ave. de la Paz 2787
Fracc. Arcos sur
Sector Juárez,
Guadalajara, Jalisco
C.P. 44500, México

### Dianetics Cultural
Association, A.C.
Carrillo Puerto
54 Bis Colonia Coyoacán
C.P. 04000, México, D.F.

### Latin American Cultural
Center, A.C.
Guanajuato #233
Colonia Roma
C.P. 06700, México, D.F.

### Institute of Applied
Philosophy, A.C.
Calle Rio Amazonas 11
Colonia Cuauhtemoc
C.P. 06500, México, D.F.

### Dianetics Technological
Institute, A.C.
Mariano Escobedo #746
Colonia Anzures
C.P. 11590, México, D.F.

### Dianetics Development
Organization, A.C.
Heriberto Frías 420
Colonia Narvarte
C.P. 03020, México, D.F.

### Dianetics Cultural
Organization, A.C.
Nicolás San Juan 1727
Colonia del Valle
C.P. 03100, México, D.F.

## Venezuela
### Dianetics Cultural
Organization, A.C.
Avenida Principal de las Palmas,
Cruce Con Calle Carúpano
Quinta Suha, Las Palmas
Caracas

### Dianetics Cultural
Association, A.C.
Avenida 101, No. 150-23
Urbanización La Alegría
Apartado Postal 833, Valencia

# CANADA

**Church of Scientology of Edmonton**
10187 112th Street
Edmonton, Alberta
Canada T5K 1M1

**Church of Scientology of Kitchener**
104 King Street West
Kitchener, Ontario
Canada N2G 2K6

**Church of Scientology of Montreal**
4489 Papineau Street
Montréal, Québec
Canada H2H 1T7

**Church of Scientology of Ottawa**
150 Rideau Street, 2nd Floor
Ottawa, Ontario
Canada K1N 5X6

**Church of Scientology of Quebec**
350 Bd Chareste Est
Québec, Québec
Canada G1K 3H5

**Church of Scientology of Toronto**
696 Yonge Street, 2nd Floor
Toronto, Ontario
Canada M4Y 2A7

**Church of Scientology of Vancouver**
401 West Hasting Street
Vancouver, British Columbia
Canada V6B 1L5

**Church of Scientology of Winnipeg**
388 Donald Street, Suite 210
Winnipeg, Manitoba
Canada R3B 2J4

## CELEBRITY CENTRES

**Church of Scientology Celebrity Centre International**
5930 Franklin Avenue
Hollywood, California 90028

**Church of Scientology Celebrity Centre Dallas**
10500 Steppington Drive, Suite 100
Dallas, Texas 75230

**Church of Scientology Celebrity Centre Las Vegas**
1100 South 10th Street
Las Vegas, Nevada 89104

**Bridge Publications, Inc.**
4751 Fountain Ave., Los Angeles, CA 90029
ISBN 0-88404-918-3

**NEW ERA Publications International ApS**
Store Kongensgade 55, 1264 Copenhagen K, Denmark
ISBN 87-7816-111-8

An L. RON HUBBARD Publication

**Church of Scientology Celebrity Centre Nashville**
1503 16th Ave. So.
Nashville, Tennessee 37212

**Church of Scientology Celebrity Centre New York**
65 East 82nd Street
New York City, New York 10028

**Church of Scientology Celebrity Centre Portland**
709 Southwest Salmon Street
Portland, Oregon 97205

**Church of Scientology Celebrity Centre London**
27 Westbourne Grove
London, England W2 4UA

**Church of Scientology Celebrity Centre Vienna**
Senefeldergasse 11/5
1100 Wien, Austria

**Church of Scientology Celebrity Centre Paris**
69, rue Legendre
75017 Paris, France

**Church of Scientology Celebrity Centre Düsseldorf**
Luisenstraße 23
40215 Düsseldorf, Germany

**Church of Scientology Celebrity Centre Florence**
Via Silvestrina 12, 1st floor
50100 Firenze, Italy

## SCIENTOLOGY MISSIONS

### INTERNATIONAL OFFICE

Scientology Missions International
6331 Hollywood Boulevard, Suite 501
Los Angeles, California 90028

▲ Scientology Missions
International Expansion Office
210 South Fort Harrison Avenue
Clearwater, Florida 34616

### WESTERN UNITED STATES

▲ Scientology Missions
International
Western United States Office
1307 N. New Hampshire, Suite 101
Los Angeles, California 90027

### EASTERN UNITED STATES

▲ Scientology Missions
International
Eastern United States Office
349 W. 48th Street
New York City, New York 10036

### UNITED KINGDOM

▲ Scientology Missions
International
United Kingdom Office
Saint Hill Manor
East Grinstead, West Sussex
England RH19 4JY

### EUROPE

▲ Scientology Missions
International
European Office
Store Kongensgade 55
1264 Copenhagen K
Denmark

▲ Scientology Missions
International
Italian Office
Via Torino, 51
Cernusco Sul Naviglio
20063 Milano, Italy

### AFRICA

▲ Scientology Missions
International
African Office
Security Building, 4th Floor
95 Commissioner Street
Johannesburg 2001
Republic of South Africa

### AUSTRALIA, NEW ZEALAND AND OCEANIA

▲ Scientology Missions
International
Australian, New Zealand and
Oceanian Office
201 Castlereagh Street
Sydney, New South Wales 2000
Australia

### LATIN AMERICA

▲ Scientology Missions
International
Latin American Office
Federación Mexicana de Dianética
Avenida Montevideo 486
Colonia Linda Vista
C.P. 07300
Mexico, D.F.

### CANADA

▲ Scientology Missions
International
Canadian Office
696 Yonge Street
Toronto, Ontario
Canada M4Y 2A7

### COMMONWEALTH OF INDEPENDENT STATES

▲ Scientology Missions
International
Commonwealth of
Independent States Office
Hubbard Humanitarian Center
Borisa Galushkina, 19-A
Moscow, Russia

## INTERNATIONAL HUBBARD ECCLESIASTICAL LEAGUE OF PASTORS

### INTERNATIONAL OFFICE

6331 Hollywood Boulevard,
Suite 901
Los Angeles, California 90028
Telephone: 213-960-3560
US & Canada: 1-800-HELP-4-YU

### WESTERN UNITED STATES

▲ Continental Liaison Office
Western United States
1308 L. Ron Hubbard Way
Los Angeles, California 9002

### EASTERN UNITED STATES

▲ Continental Liaison Office
Eastern United States
349 W. 48th Street
New York City, New York 100

### UNITED KINGDOM

▲ Continental Liaison Office
United Kingdom
Saint Hill Manor
East Grinstead, West Sussex
England RH19 4JY

### CANADA

▲ Continental Liaison Office
Canada
696 Yonge Street
Toronto, Ontario
Canada M4Y 2A7

### AFRICA

▲ Continental Liaison Office A
6th Floor, Budget House
130 Main Street
Johannesburg 2001
Republic of South Africa

### LATIN AMERICA

▲ Continental Liaison Office
Latin America
Federación Mexicana de Dianética
Pomona #53
Colonia Roma
C.P. 06700, México, D.F.

### AUSTRALIA, NEW ZEALAND AND OCEANIA

▲ Continental Liaison Office A
201 Castlereagh Street, 3rd
Sydney, New South Wales 20
Australia

### EUROPE

▲ Continental Liaison Office
Europe
Store Kongensgade 55
1264 Copenhagen K
Denmark